Eat Like Eve

Irresistible Recipes for Nude Food

by Cherry Capri

Gluten Free!
Dairy Free & Vegan!
Live FUN Raw Foodstuff!

Published by
Futura House
2620 South Maryland Parkway #345
Las Vegas, NV 89109
Printed in the United States of America
Cover photo and all additional photos of Cherry Capri
by Julie Klima (julieklima.com)
Cherry Capri illustration image by SHAG (shag.com)
Book Design, Food Photography & Illustrations
by MM Stratton (megorama.com)

Disclaimer: This book is sold for information purposes only. This book is not intended a medical, physical or dental advice either directly or indirectly, because the authors and the publishers of this work are not medical doctors. The intent of the author is to information is of a general entertaining nature to help you in your quest for fun and spiritual well-being. In the event you use any of the information in this book for yourself, which is your constitutional right, neither the author nor the publisher will be held accountable and assume no responsibility for your actions, adverse effects or consequences of any kind resulting from the use or misuse of any suggestions or procedures described hereafter.

Library of Congress Cataloging-in-Publication Data
Capri, Cherry, 1969-
Eat Like Eve: Irresistible Recipes for Nude Food / Capri, Cherry
Summary: "In Eat Like Eve, Cherry Capri maintains that Eve in the Garden of Eden looked great, because she was eating a raw, plant-based diet. Cherry explains the equipment and ingredients of raw food and shares 88 quick delicious vegan, dairy free, gluten free recipes." - Provided by the publisher.
ISBN 978-0-9965835-0-3 (soft cover color)
ISBN: 978-0-9965835-1-0 (kindle)
ISBN: 978-0-9965835-2-7 (nook)
ISBN: 978-0-9965835-3-4 (audio)
ISBN 978-0-9965835-4-1 (CreateSpace soft cover black & white)
Raw food diet ›Recipes
Cookbooks, Food & Wine › Cooking Methods › Raw
Cookbooks, Food & Wine › Special Diet › Vegetarian & Vegan
Health, Fitness & Dieting › Diets & Weight Loss › Other Diets
Healthy Desserts
First Printing. July 2015

Contents

Crusts of Bread & Such 43

Salads, Sides & Sustenance................ 49

Drinks & Smoothies 75

Postscript 81

Resources 85

Index 86

Dedication

This book is dedicated to gardeners, growers and seed savers everywhere.

It is dedicated to the stalwart farmers who cultivate organic and veganic gardens.

And lastly, it is dedicated to the wonderful people who raise heirloom produce. These are people of outstanding character, horticultural excellence and divine beauty who should be thanked profusely for keeping our agricultural heritage alive. Thank You!

Eat Like Eve by Cherry Capri

Introduction

Eve was the ultimate woman wasn't she? After her, they broke the mold. When you think about it, she was the original 'bad girl.' I mean, look at the company she hung out with? Hunky Adam hanging out in the altogether! And then there's that other "horny" guy that was in the garden, too. Yet, she was also the mother of humanity, so there must have been some nurturing and nesting Martha Stewart in her, too.

One of the main things she had going for her, though, was her diet. In the beginning, she was running around Eden naked as a jay bird. And

> **"Eat dead foods...**
> **You will look like**
> **a deadbeat!"**

later, she was still only covered in fig leaves. "Girlfriend" must-a had a hot body and some fierce self-confidence being half dressed all the time!

But seriously, how could you not look great if all you ate were fresh raw uncooked organic fruits and vegetables? That's the whole point of the Raw Food diet. Simply put: eat dead flesh and dead cooked foods and you will have lousy energy and look like a deadbeat. Eat living foods and you will look great and feel more alive and vibrant!

That's how I got started on this way of life. My world was moving so fast. I've gotta Lotta Living to do! I needed to figure out a way to keep the pounds off and keep my energy up, up, up! That's when my friend Matthew introduced me to David Wolfe's book called the Eating for Beauty.

This book made me think completely differently about the food I ate.

Somewhere along the line, some smarty pants figured out that, although the vitamins and minerals remain intact after food is cooked, the enzymes that keep them 'lively' in a matter of speaking, are basically killed when you heat things above a certain temperature. (Roughly above 118 degrees in wet heat and about 150 degrees in dry heat). That actually makes sense when you think about it. Plants and animals aren't so different. Living creatures certainly can't stay alive in super high temperatures. The main thing is: our body requires lots of live juicy enzymes to stay healthy and happy.

So like so many of us, I've always considered myself to be a reasonably healthy eater. I was a vegetarian for years and that should have put me ahead of the curve, right? Well, although I got all of my basic servings of fruits and veggies each day, I still was cooking the enzymes right out of everything. And I was eating way too many pastas, breads, baked desserts and cheating with cheeses. Ahead of the curve? I was getting curvier and curvier!!!

> "Ahead of the curve?
> Well... I *was* getting curvier!"

I found that I wanted to eat raw, but I am also a flavor addict. Simple salads weren't enough for me. I love to eat yummy things. Doesn't everybody? I like to experiment in the kitchen, but at the same time, I don't want to be a slave to it either. It seemed like many raw food chefs WERE slaves to their kitchens. The recipes had long lists of ingredients and a thousand and one steps.

So I started monkeying around with existing raw recipes and began to develop my own set of simple "quick fix" versions of old standbys.

> "I was addicted to the sentimental associations of cooked foods."

The end result is this book which is filled with recipes that avoid complicated or multi-step processes.

I also desperately needed to create recipes based on the cooked foods I missed emotionally. (That is a big part of eating raw food, by the way...) I was literally addicted to sentimental associations with certain foods. Not just the tastes and flavors, but I was addicted to the emotions of eating potato salad and fried veggie chicken in the summer and hot soup or fresh warm brownies on a cold rainy day. Overcoming that emotional addiction can be even harder than changing your physical diet.

For me, it was all or nothing at all. I took the plunge to go 100% - what they call "high raw." I felt great! My energy multiplied exponentially. My skin tone brightened up and a few stray grey hairs even turned bright red again. (Really - it's all natural color darlings - just like Lucille Ball!) Eventually, I started to eat more seasonally, which meant adding in a few cooked foods - especially during the winter months when some fresh foods are tougher to find. I have since taken a sensible and realistic approach. I now eat about 70-90% raw foods, supplementing with cooked foods when it is convenient to do so and as the seasons change.

Now, I am NOT suggesting you do the same. And don't get worried about giving up your favorite foods cold turkey for this diet. All I AM asking, is that you take a pause and think about what you put in your mouth before you put it in there.

I.e. think twice about that piece o' pie you are about to cram into your pie-hole. Try to include more living foods that help keep you alive!

As mentioned, I have many wonderful Raw Food Cookbooks with great recipes by incredibly talented chefs. However, they are often filled with complicated multi-step procedures. THIS IS NOT one of those books. You are not expected to make an entire raw meal. This book is designed to help you learn to make one little recipe at a time. The idea is to help you find one or two simple easy raw alternatives to a few favorite foods. And it's geared to help you gain confidence as you go.

> "Think twice about that piece o' pie
> you are about to cram
> into your pie-hole!"

Take your time. Transition little by little. For me, having a handful of favorite basic recipes I could count on to inspire me made it easier. Hopefully they will do the same for you.

Sure, things might taste a little different or even 'weird' at first, but you'll get used to the new way of doing things and I will lay odds that you will end up liking the new way even better... especially knowing how great you will feel in the long run.

After all, we are all just angels lost in our little Garden of Eden planet trying to wake up and create some heaven on earth. So keep it simple. And guess what? It's okay to have fun and play with your food.

Eat more living foods and live better.

Step up to that tree and...

EAT THAT APPLE!

Acknowledgements

Thank you to Chef Mason for his master culinary support and to Anand who provided both editing and sound nutritional advice. Thank you to David Wolfe and all of the RAWk stars of the Living Food movement who have inspired me. A big thank you to all of the raw food devotees who share on social media on a regular basis. You come up with so many great ideas that keep us all enthused! Keep Sharing!

Thank you to Markus. He was my first...
...person who gave me raw chocolate many years ago, that is.

Thank you to Jay and MiShell Nailor for their artistic support and for their son, Matthew who has been my go-to raw food guru.

Thanks to <u>CA Modern Magazine</u> along with <u>Tiki Magazine</u> and <u>Java's Bachelor Pad Magazine</u> for being the first to put my advice and recipes into actual print. Hold onto back issues folks!

Thank you to Queen Skittles for being such a flamboyant photographer and to King James for being chief Palm Tree Wrangler!

I would like to thank Kay Lovelace, whom I have never met, but for her inspiration. She illustrated so many of my favorite vintage Culinary Arts Cookbooks from the 1950s.

I would also like to thank the various esoteric instructors I have had throughout my journey and to Rich Million for keeping me on my toes.

Lastly, thanks to my creative director/editor identical cousin m&m without whom, I could not get half my work done.

The Basics

In the beginning, a couple was hanging out in the garden and said, "Let there be parties." And there were seed-bearing plants on the face of the whole earth and there were trees that had fruit with seeds in them. They were theirs for food. And man created cocktail elixirs out of juices and herbs and woman created canapés out of nuts and seeds. And they tasted them and they saw that they were good.

In this garden, there was a tree of knowledge of cooking and artificial additives. After a few cocktails, eventually people got bold and curious about that tree. And well, things got messed up. They learned about cooking and that made them eat foods they weren't supposed to eat. And the artificial ingredients made them lazy. Some folks added artificial flavors and colors to the cocktails

and preservatives to now-cooked canapés!
My stars! Nothing tasted the real anymore.
And they didn't feel very good the day after they
imbibed and ate.

Nowadays, anyone with any common sense should
be looking for options to bring back 'real' flavor and
better health. So I invite you to rediscover "Original
Foods," fresh from the garden.

"Slow and steady progress on your path
helps you make great strides
towards big goals."

Take Baby Steps!

I myself maintain a mostly raw vegetarian diet.
However, I am less concerned with convincing
you to go 100% raw vegan. Rather, start thinking
about how you can eat a little lower on the food
chain and adding more fresh veggies to that burger,
pasta dish or on top of that pizza..

I am convinced that you'll get lots of health benefits
from switching from the Standard American Diet
(SAD) to more of a vegetarian diet. But by going a
step even further into raw foods, you can retain
even *more* antioxidants, enzymes and other
beneficial compounds. Just take little baby steps.
Slow and steady progress on your path helps you
make great strides towards big goals. This kind of
approach works for me. I admire folks who can dive
into the deep end of the pool. But *this* girl likes to
dangle in a toe at a time and test the water little by
little. You can do that, too!

Raw Food Enzymes in a Nutshell

Okay - so what's all this fuss about enzymes?
We need bacteria, probiotics and enzymes to live
healthfully. Enzymes are complex proteins that act
as catalysts in numerous body processes. Over
5000 enzymes have been identified today. Dr.
Edward Howell, a noted pioneer in the field
of enzyme research wrote back at the beginning of
the 20th century that a diet composed of cooked
foods puts a strain on the pancreas and other
organs, resulting in poor resistance to stress and a
shortened life span. His research found that most
enzymes are deactivated at
a wet-heat temperature of around 118 degrees
Fahrenheit, and a dry-heat temperature of about
150 degrees. Seeds seem to be more tolerant of
heating than other fresh foods.

Supplies

There are numerous books and websites available
that will tell you in detail about the various types of
machines and equipment you'll need to prepare raw
food, so I won't go into that kind of detail here. But I
will give you a list of the equipment I used to create
all the recipes in this book. Yes, many of these items
can be pricey, but when you think about it... how
much did you spend on your coffee maker, blender,
toaster, microwave, grill-master, etc.? And if you
own a home - how much did your wall oven and
stovetop cost?

When you put these things into context -
raw food preparation equipment isn't so pricey
after all. Plus, if you are eating healthier, think
of the potential aches 'n pains and bills you won't
pay for in future years! So here are some items
you're going to need:

High Speed Blender

While a high end piece of machinery like a juicer is super swell to have, a solid high-speed blender will get you through most recipes just fine. I have used a good ole fashioned 1960s Osterizer blender for many of these recipes, but you will find that a high speed blender will work much better for recipes involving blending nuts and seeds. I personally own a VitaMix brand blender and love it. You will also need a food processor eventually, but get the blender first.

Dehydrator

I did also splurge on two additional expensive items: an old fashioned stand mixer and a dehydrator. I started off with a smaller round dehydrator (the kind you see at the home improvement shows) but quickly realized, there was no temperature gauge on it and it was overheating my food in the center and not dehydrating enough around the edges. I quickly invested in a large multi-tray unit with temperature control and it has made my life so much easier.

You will see me mention "teflex" over and over... it's a non-stick sheet that goes into your dehydrator. You can use good old fashioned parchment paper, as well.

Regarding dehydration times and temperatures. This book is about making it 'easy' and not complicated. I turn my dehydrator on to about 115 degrees whenever I use it. I turn it on and forget about it. There are different schools of thought that say you can turn the temperature up higher for the first half hour or so to speed up

"I turn it on and forget it."

processing time, but then what happens if you forget to turn the temp down?
You will defeat the whole point of raw dehydration. So Keep It Simple Sweety.

Also regarding times to dehydrate. I have put suggested times in some recipes, but these may vary depending on how wet your mixtures are.
As you will be dealing with natural foods that will have variety in terms of size and volume, it is not an exact science. Some lemons are simply bigger and wetter than others.

> "As a former oven-burning baker,
> I love this about raw food!"

However, dehydration is a pretty forgiving process. Generally if you leave things in for an extra hour or two, it shouldn't make too much of
a difference. So just keep an eye on your projects as you go, and eventually you'll get a sense of the correct timing. As a former oven-burning baker, I love this about raw food! You'll never need oven mitts or risk burning yourself (or set off smoke alarms) again!

Food Processor

For most of my sauces and quick mixes I use a food processor. If you cannot afford one of those right away, they also make less expensive attachments that fit right on top of your existing blender.
I have one of those, too. No, it can't make super large batches of things like a full size processor. But I like it just the same. It's compact and
easy-to-clean. Someday, maybe you'll invest in a major 14 cup sized gizmo, when you throw your first raw food party! But for now a little tabletop two cup vessel works just fine.

Storage

As far as storage times go, try to keep things fresh. You know inherently what that means. If you make up snacks or have leftovers and you plan on keeping them around for a day or two, refrigeration or freezing might be in order. Use your common sense. Also, please invest in some decent glass or ceramic containers to store your sauces and dressings, rather than plastic.

Finances

I might hear you grumbling, "But all of these fancy ingredients and equipment are *Expensive!*" My answer is this: Would you rather budget your money a bit and splurge $50 on this or that, or spend $100's on health expenses in the future? I like my doctor a lot, but frankly, I would rather spend the money on raw chocolate now, than on her time later. Quite simply, and generally speaking, the healthier you eat, the more likely you are to be a healthy person.

If you are really under tight economic circumstances, there are always workarounds. Before I had a dehydrator, I tried to use my oven at its lowest temperature with the door open. But that is NOT energy efficient and the money you'd lose on that practice will pay for your dehydrator.

Another example of thriftiness is Food Network star Alton Brown actually described how to make a cheap MacGyver style dehydrator out of a fan, bungee cords and some cotton air filters. (Google it.) It was very clever, but also potentially messy, time intensive, and in the long-run, quite wasteful, because you would have to keep buying replacement air filters. So do yourself a favor and invest in the real thing as soon as you are able to. Your time and life is more valuable than money!

Ingredients

I have tried to base these recipes around things you will be more familiar with: like common fruits, vegetables, nuts and seeds. But there may be some new exotic foods you will hear mentioned throughout the rest of the book. Some are not 100% raw, but they have enough benefits to make them a valuable part of a raw diet approach.
Most of these ingredients will be readily available in your local health food store or online.

There are plenty of books and websites dedicated to super-foods, like goji berries, acai, sea vegetables, etc., so I will focus on some of my personal favorites and what is used in the recipes.

General Guidelines

> "Please favor organically grown items for recipes..."

Make sure you start looking at labels a little more closely, okay? There are plenty of items on the grocery shelves labeled "all natural" but that doesn't mean they haven't been processed. For instance, with agave and honey, there are both raw versions and NOT raw versions of these. So READ labels. Even Turbinado sugar and Sucanat, which are often labeled "raw" or less-processed, they are technically not raw. They are heat processed.

Your oils should be "Cold Pressed" and your nuts and seeds labeled raw, not blanched, baked, cooked or roasted. Harder to find in the stores are things like Nama Shoyu ('raw' soy sauce), but you can find them online.

Finally, I cannot stress enough how important it is to please favor organically grown items for these recipes. This is not just for health sake, but for overall planetary health. We all have to start making more decisions that benefit humanity and our beautiful little Garden of Eden earth. If you are concerned about higher prices of organic items, I do commiserate. But still, please read my notes (two pages ago) about finances again!

Agave Nectar & Sweeteners

Humans crave sweet substances because we use sugar for energy. The rawest of sugar to use for most recipes is blended pitted dates, but sometimes the texture, blend-a-bility and/or flavor they impart is not quite right for a dish.

Agave is a commercially produced sweetener that comes from the Agave cactus plant. It is processed sugar, but I use it because it is relatively easy to find and blends very well. It also does not add any particular flavor other than 'sweetness.' It is supposed to be lower on the glycemic

> "Grade B maple syrup is a good sweetener to try."

index than highly refined sugars which means that, when ingested it converts into sugar in your body at a slower rate. That's sounds to me like it would be better for your health. There are both regular (refined) and raw versions of agave, so make sure you chose RAW. Other good sweeteners are locally-sourced Raw Honey (not vegan) and good old fashioned Date Sugar, Date Syrup or Coconut Syrup. But these can get pricey. If you are diabetic, research Yacon Syrup. Maple Syrup is also a good sweetener to try when you can't find the others. Buy Grade "B" because it is more nutrient dense and mineral rich.

Apple Cider Vinegar

Most vinegars are highly processed and distilled with no real health benefits, however cider vinegar is made from fermented apples with many living nutrients left intact. It is used in many old folk remedies. Choose organic, unfiltered and un-pasteurized. I will tell you that sometimes I will simply substitute lemon juice when a recipe calls for vinegar. And guess what - you can do that, too!

Blue Green Algae, Spirulina, Chlorella, Green Powders

I lump all of these algae-type products into a category of food I affectionately call 'pond scum!" Humans have been consuming algae for hundreds if not thousands, of years for health benefits. It is the most ancient of superfoods filled with protein, phytochemicals, vitamins and minerals. Buy powder, then you can slip a little bit into any number of these recipes to get additional nutrient density. And that will hide the algae flavor.

Brewer's and Nutritional Yeast

This is different from active bread yeast. This is a yeast that has potentially good things for your insides. It is an excellent source of B vitamins and amino acids (aka protein). It also lends a cheesy flavor, especially when mixed with lemon. Brewer's Yeast is a byproduct of the beer industry. Nutritional Yeast is generally grown on molasses. You may find that Brewer's Yeast has a bitter flavor, so I prefer Nutritional Yeast, but you can use either one when a recipe calls for 'yeast.'

> "Theobromine Cacao literally means, 'Food of the Gods.' And why, yes, it is!"

Cacao

Cacao is the raw seed form of Cocoa (chocolate) without all the milk, refined sugars and other bad additives. If you eat chocolate made with raw cacao and raw sweeteners - you will never have to feel guilty again. It's so yummy and can be good for you that you'll want to eat things called, "life by chocolate." The scientific name for the plant is Theobroma Cacao and literally means, "Food of the Gods." And why yes, it is!

Raw Carob powder is often used as a substitute for cacao powder. I actually use it as an additive, because carob provides calcium to the high magnesium content cacao and helps to balance it.

> "While I adore the pink color,
> I steer clear of eating rocks and crystals..."

Celtic Sea Salt

Common salt is mined, processed, iodized, bleached and has chemicals and anti-caking agents added to it. Any beneficial minerals and trace elements are practically gone by the time it reaches your table. Some table salts are just chemical by-products! You will also see some fancy pants pink salt, and while I adore the pink color, I steer clear of eating rock salts and crystals. (I keep those on my desk to hold down papers!) I personally do not think they are absorbed easily by the body and sea salt is better. Celtic Sea Salt or French grey sea salt is considered to be one of the best. It is living nutritious food, hand harvested and sun-dried on the pristine coast of Northern France.

Distilled Water

For any recipe involving water, I only use pure water. If you have access to a freshwater spring with low TDS (Total Dissolved Solids) by all means use that! Since I am not always spring-adjacent, I use 100% steam distilled water. It is the purest H_2O you can find. Just please remember to use pure water for everything you ingest - and that includes when you soak your nuts.

Flax Seed

Meat proponents will say you get your essential Omega 3 fatty acids from animal and fish sources. You can get them from flax seeds, meal and oil, too. And they have found them in some seaweeds.

Honey

Some vegans eschew honey being that is animal-produced food. I eat it sparingly. But I buy from local~ farmers who maintain humane practices with their bees. Raw honey is a great immunity booster, a natural remedy for many ailments, plus it's a great source of pure sun-based energy. Again though, please make sure you get the raw kind. And try to develop a relationship with a local beekeeper and support their bee friendly business.

Maca

Maca is a root from South America that is great for balancing your hormones and is thought to be an aphrodisiac. Not only that, it has a really pleasant unusual flavor. I like to put it in anything chocolate because they go together so well.

Nama Shoyu

Soy Sauce is made from fermenting soy beans. Normal soy sauce has been heat pasteurized and loses all of its beneficial nutrients. But "nama" literally means raw, fresh or uncooked. Which is why some raw foodists also drink "nama" sake! Imagine that? Raw wine!!! If you are allergic to wheat, you can get wheat-free soy sauce, or if you are soy intolerant, you can substitute 1 tbsp. of salt to 1/2 cup water. Lastly, for all soy products, please support the non-GMO (genetically modified organism) soy products. Bragg's makes a soy-based soy sauce replacement called Liquid Aminos which is not raw - but it is labeled as non-GMO.
If you can't find nama shoyu, you can use this.

Raw Olive Oil

Always buy Extra Virgin, organic and first cold pressed, but also try to find a label that states that they cold press their olives at a temperature below 100 degrees F. Also look for "Stone crushed" or "No heat is used to extract" and "unfiltered."

Soy Lecithin

It's not raw, but lecithin powder is used as an optional thickening agent and emulsifier. It also lends some health benefits of soy. Here, I ALWAYS buy an organic non-genetically modified variety.

Raw Nuts and Seeds

Make sure you get raw nuts and seeds and not roasted salted varieties. You really should "pre-soak" your nuts and seeds for all of the recipes. No, you don't absolutely have to pre-soak, but if you can make the time, please please do it.

Nuts have phytic acid which makes them difficult to digest and leads to mineral deficiencies. Soaking them help wash that away. Soaking also helps to deactivate enzyme inhibitors that they contain... again making them easier to digest. Soaking also makes them blend more smoothly.

Different nuts require different soak times depending on how hard or dense the nut is. For instance, almonds should ideally soak overnight or longer, while cashews only require a couple of hours for optimization. And always soak your nuts in pure, preferably distilled or Spring water. Why? Because they are 'soaking' up the water. You don't want nuts with chlorine or tap water chemicals in them, do you now? I thought not.

"Give your nuts a hot bath. It might help."

Here is info on the nuts mentioned in this book:

Almonds: 7-12 hours soak - 12 hour to sprout

Cashews: 2-4 hours - does not sprout

Macadamia Nuts: 7 hours - does not sprout

Pecans: 3-4 hours - does not sprout

Pine Nuts: do not soak - does not sprout

Pistachio: do not soak - does not sprout

Pumpkin Seeds: 7-8 hours soak - 1-2 days to sprout

Sesame Seeds: 8 hours soak - 1-2 days to sprout

Sunflower Seeds: 2 hours soak - 2-3 days to sprout

Walnuts: 3-4 hours soak - does not sprout

Please discard the soak water.

Sometimes if you are in a hurry and/or forgot
to soak your nuts, give your nuts a hot bath.
It might help in a pinch. Yes, literally dunk your nuts
in some very hot water for a short while.
It may deactivate at least some of the enzyme
inhibitors. This is quite effective for almonds.
And at the very least it will make them more
easily blended.

Now you are armed with a little knowledge...
Let's Eat Like Eve!

Snack?

Did Somebody Say Snack?

In my humble opinion, good snacks are the most important part of starting a new way of eating. Let's face it, your body's taste buds are going to freak out a bit and get hungry for familiar tastes at odd times. Trust me. Your brain will remember how it loved pizza. At that point - be strong. Have scrumptious raw Pizzy Bites on hand and eat them instead. Give your craving a day or two after eating the raw version. THEN I dare you to eat a pizza. It won't taste quite as good as you remembered. That's because you are re-training your brain to enjoy live natural foods and flavor, and not crave empty calories and fat.

I make up batches of snacks and then keep them in the fridge or freezer. They're great to bring along on road trips or when you're out 'n' about and you know you might want a snack later.

Be a Raw Whiz!
Cheezy Chips

- 1 cup macadamia nuts
- 1 cup cashews
- 1 red bell pepper
- 1 lime (trim rind)
- salt to taste

→ Combine all ingredients in a food processor and blend until reasonably smooth.

→ Place tbsp. of the mixture on teflex sheet in dehydrator.

→ Dehydrate 6-8 hours.

→ Flip over when tops are dry so undersides get dehydrated, also.

Presto Pesto!
Pesto Pine Nuts

- 1 cup pine nuts
- 1 tbsp. finely minced/ pureed fresh garlic or garlic powder
- 5-6 basil leaves
- 1 tbsp. water
- 1 tsp. salt

→ Finely mince basil.

→ Toss everything in a giant bowl.

→ Marinate for an hour or more.

→ Spread out nuts on a teflex sheet.

→ Dehydrate overnight.

TIP:
Dried herbs will have a more concentrated flavor, so if you are using fresh herbs, don't be afraid to add a little extra in.

Chilly My Soul
Chili Pistachios

- 16 oz. bag raw shelled pistachios (yes, you'll want to do the WHOLE bag)
- juice of 1 lime
- 2 tbsp. chili powder
- 1 tbsp. onion powder
- pinch of cayenne (more for spicy)
- ½ tsp. salt

→ Throw everything into bowl and get everything coated.
→ Marinate overnight.
→ Spread out on a teflex tray and dehydrate overnight.

Suggestions

Serve as a party or travel snack.
Use as a taco 'meat' substitute!

Jive Turkey
Turkey Nuggets

- 2 cups walnuts
- 2 cups almonds
- 1 cup parsley
- 1 onion
- 6 stalks celery
- 2 tbsp. each: garlic powder, sage, rosemary, thyme
- 2 tbsp. nama shoyu

→ Combine all ingredients in the food processor and blend until reasonably smooth.
→ Place tbsp. of the mixture on teflex sheet in dehydrator.
→ Dehydrate 6-8 hours.
→ Halfway through the dehydration, flip over and flatten out so undersides are dehydrated, also.

Golden Un-fried Nuggets
Chicky Nuggets

- 1 cup cashews
- 1 tomato
- 2 cloves garlic
- ½ cup shredded coconut
- ½ sweet onion
- salt & pepper to taste

→ Combine ingredients in food processor and blend until smooth.

→ Place tbsp. of the mixture on teflex sheet in dehydrator.

→ Dehydrate one day.

→ Flip over when tops are dry so undersides get dehydrated, also.

Suggestion

Additional herbs and spices to mix in include: celery salt, sage and thyme.

Chippity Do Dah
Pizzy Bites

- 1 cup cashews
- 1 tomato
- 6 sun-dried tomatoes
- 2 tbsp. agave
- 1 tbsp. oregano
- 2 cloves garlic
- 1 tsp. yeast
- salt to taste

→ Soak sun-dried tomatoes for ten minutes and drain.

→ Combine ingredients in the food processor and blend until smooth.

→ Place tbsp. on teflex sheet in dehydrator.

→ Dehydrate one day.

→ Halfway through dehydration - flip over, flatten out so undersides dry also.

Suggestion

Reserve one or two dried tomatoes. Micro-dice and press them into bites midway through dehydrating.

Be Mine
Bar-B-Que Chips

- 1 cup cashews
- 1 tomato
- ½ onion
- ½ cup agave
- 1 lemon (cut off rind)
- 1 tbsp. vinegar
- 1 tsp. chili powder
- 1 tsp. smoked paprika
- salt to taste

→ Combine ingredients in the food processor and blend until reasonably smooth.

→ Place tbsp. of the mixture on teflex sheet in dehydrator.

→ Dehydrate one day.

→ Halfway through dehydration, flip over and flatten out so undersides are dehydrated, also.

Swell Stuff
Kale Chips

- 1 head of kale (curly or flat) torn so tough middle veins are removed
- 1 cup Heavenly Ginger Dressing (Page 32)

→ Tear up kale leaves.

→ Put in a big baggie to coat the leaves completely (just like Shake and Bake!). Or you can mix in a big bowl.

→ Place dressing soaked leaves of kale on teflex trays.

→ Dehydrate one day.

→ Flip leaves halfway through.

Suggestion

You can make a variation of Kale Chips using cheezy sauces or pretty much any sauce that suits you.

Grandola
Breakfast Bars

- **1 part sunflower seeds**
- **1 part flax meal**
- **1 part agave**
- **1 part gogi berries**
- **1 part raisins**
- **1 part almonds**

→ Soak gogi berries, raisins for an hour or more before mixing.

→ Smash the almond with a mallet so they are slightly crushed.

→ Combine ingredients.

→ Spread on teflex sheet.

→ Dehydrate one day.

On Yonder
Onion Rings

- **1 small onion**
- **½ cup nama shoyu**
- **½ cup flax meal**
- **½ cup yeast**

→ Slice onion thin and soak in Nama Shoyu in refrigerator overnight.

→ Mix flax and yeast in a bowl and add any additional seasonings you like.

→ Roll soaked onions in flax yeast mixture and then place on dehydrator trays.

→ Dehydrate one day.

→ Flip halfway through.

Suggestion
Keep mints handy!

Eat Like Eve by Cherry Capri

Saucy Dips 'n' Dressings

I have always maintained that the major part
of cooking is what we put on *top* of things.
Our addictions to meat and cooked foods are very
much based on our love of flavor: the spices and
especially, the sauces!

So always have a favorite dressing or sauce on
hand and you will never go hungry. For instance,
Mom's Movie Star Sauce is my all-time favorite.
I can put it on top of some plain ole kale and have
a veritable feast. Or I can put this incredible
dressing over a *baked* potato - and still have
the benefits of raw enzymes along with my
not-so-alive food.

Learn how to whip up a dressing or two and you will
have gained one of the secret ingredients
of raw chef mastery.

Mom's Movie Star Sauce
Ginger Dressing

- ¾ cup olive oil
- ½ cup nama shoyu
- 4 cloves garlic
- 2-3 thumbs of ginger
- 2-3 lemons (trim rind)
- ground pepper to taste

→ Blend all ingredients in a high speed blender.

Suggestions

Serve over cooked foods like potatoes to add living enzymes to them.

Serve liberally on a head of curly kale. (Tear up the leaves and remove the stems). →

Let kale marinate for a few hours in a bowl in the fridge for softer kale leaves.

Top it All Off
Nutty Topping

- 1 cup walnuts
- 1 cup sunflower seeds
- ¾ cup yeast
- 1 tsp. salt

→ Pulse in food processor until not quite smooth.

Suggestion

Use in lieu of Parmesan Cheese for topping salads or pastas.

Everybody Needs a Salad Sometime

Basic Italian Dressing

- **1 cup olive oil**
- **1 lemon (seeded and peel trimmed off) OR ½ cup vinegar**
- **pinch of garlic powder**
- **pinch of oregano**
- **salt & pepper to taste**

→ Blend all ingredients until smooth.

Suggestions

Serve over crisp lettuce with some sliced tomatoes and a pepperoncini (not raw) on the side.

Serve over Bok Choy!

For a Greek Dressing, add more oregano and some mustard and serve on a Greek Salad (Page 53).

TIP:
Of course the most appropriate raw vinegar is lemon juice. But if you don't have a lemon handy, the next best choice is unfiltered Apple Cider Vinegar.

DRESSING ROOM

What a Tomato!
Chunky Checca

- 3 Roma tomatoes
- 2 tbsp. olive oil
- 3 cloves garlic
- 6-8 fresh basil leaves
- salt to taste

→ Dice up your tomatoes, garlic and basil leaves.

→ Mix ingredients.

Suggestions

Serve on raw Garlic Bread (Page 46) to make raw Bruschetta! Serve over pasta.

Seize Her!
Caesar Dressing

- ¾ cup olive oil
- ⅓ cup water
- ⅓ cup pine nuts
- ¼ cup vinegar
- ½ lemon (trim rind)
- ¼ small onion
- 2 tbsp. nama shoyu
- 1 tbsp. oregano
- 1 tbsp. lecithin (optional thickener)
- 3 cloves garlic
- salt to taste

→ Rough chop onion and marinate in nama shoyu for minimum of one hour.

→ Blend everything in a high speed blender until smooth.

Suggestions

Serve over romaine lettuce topped with raw Croutons. (Page 46) and Nutty Topping (Page 32). Add ⅛ sheet raw nori into blended dressing for extra fishy flavor.

Eat Like Eve by Cherry Capri

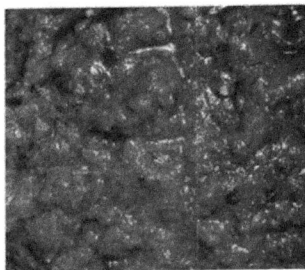

I wish you the Merriest, Merriest
Marinara Sauce

- 3 tomatoes
- 1 cup sun-dried tomatoes
- ½ cup juice of a lemon
- 2 tbsp. nama shoyu
- 2 tbsp. olive oil
- ½ yellow onion
- 3 cloves garlic

→ Soak sun-dried tomatoes for ten minutes and drain water.
Reserve water for blending if needed.

→ Blend all ingredients in blender until smooth.

Suggestion
Add 1 additional finely diced raw tomato to the sauce at the end.

Ah So...
Chinese Chicky Salad Dressing

- 1 cup sesame oil
- ½ cup rice wine vinegar (not raw, but we cheat for this flavor)
- 1 large thumb ginger (about 2")
- 3 tbsp. nama shoyu
- 1 clove garlic
- 2 tbsp. agave/honey

→ Blend away.

→ Garnish with raw sesame seeds.

Suggestions
Reserve some of ginger, micro-dice it, then hand blend in at end.

Serve on chopped Broccoli! Pea Pods! Cabbage! Cilantro! (Page 50).

TIP:
Raw Marinara is my favorite first-timer food to teach people how to make and to serve to raw newbies.

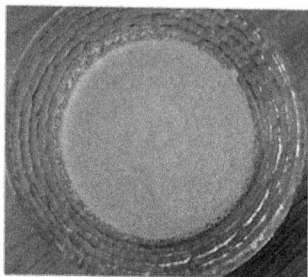

Don't Be Afraid-O
Alfredo Sauce

- ¾ cup olive oil
- ½ cup pine nuts
- ¼ cup cashews
- 4 cloves garlic
- juice of 1 lime (or lemon)
- 1 tbsp. yeast
- 1 tbsp. water
- salt to taste
- fresh ground pepper

→ Blend everything together in high speed blender.

Green Bean Dippity Do
Raw Hummus

- 2 cups raw chickpeas
- ¼ cup olive oil
- 2-3 cloves garlic
- juice of one lemon
- 1 tbsp. water (more as needed)
- pinch of cumin (or substitute with coriander)
- salt to taste

→ Blend all ingredients in high speed blender until smooth.

Suggestions

Substitute zucchini for chickpeas.
Add ¼ cup cashews for a creamier texture.
Add cayenne pepper.
Add ¼ cup softened and chopped up sun-dried tomatoes.
Add ¼ cup diced olives.
Serve with carrot sticks or endive 'chips'.

Eat Like Eve by Cherry Capri

Thai One On
Spicy Peanut Sauce

- 1 cup almond butter
- ½ cup water
- ¼ cup agave
- 1 inch of ginger
- 4 tbsp. lemon juice
- 3 tbsp. nama shoyu
- 3 tbsp. sesame oil
- 3 cloves garlic

→ Blend everything in high speed blender until smooth.

Suggestions

Add ⅛ of a seeded minced jalapeño.

Serve over chopped fresh raw veggies or check out my Pad Thai recipe (Page 52).

Make sure you purchase RAW almond butter from the store. Or you can make almond butter with soaked almonds in your high speed blender.

Salsa for Swingers
Salsa

- 3 tomatoes (heirloom tomatoes are my favorites)
- ½ cup cilantro
- ½ cup scallions
- juice of half a lemon
- splash of olive oil
- ¼ tsp. garlic and/or chili powder
- salt & pepper to taste

→ Dice tomatoes and scallions
→ Chop cilantro
→ Mix all up in a bowl

Suggestion

Serve with cabbage leaf chips.

TIP:
Any time you have raw garlic or onions around, fresh parsley is a great breath freshener.

Nice n' Spicy
Chili Salsa

- 4 ancho chilies
- 2 chipotle chilies
- ½ cup water
- ½ onion
- 1 tsp. salt
- ½ tsp. paprika
- ½ tsp. vinegar

→ Seed and
de-stem chilies.

→ Soak chilies in half cup
water for half hour.
Reserve water for
blending.

→ Blend until smooth.

Suggestion
Add fresh garlic
for extra kick!

Say Cheese!
Garlic Cream Cheese

- ½ cup cashews
- ½ tsp. yeast
- 2-3 cloves of garlic
- juice of half a lemon
- 1 tsp. salt

→ Pulse in food
processor and
blend until smooth.
Use water as needed.

Suggestion
Serve in celery sticks
or over raw crackers.

Substitute sunflower
seeds for cashews.

Instead of garlic and salt,
use 1 tbsp. of miso.

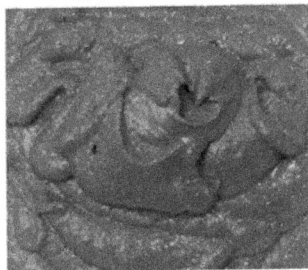

Holy Moly Batman!
Oaxaca Mole

- 3-4 chilies
  (Ancho, Pasilla,
  Poblano varieties)
- 2 avocados
- 1 large tomato
- 2 tomatillos
- ½ cup raisins
- ¼ yellow onion
- ¼ cup pumpkin seeds
- 2 cloves garlic
- 3 tablespoons raw
  cacao powder
- 1 tbsp. nama shoyu
- ½ tsp. each: oregano,
  cumin, cinnamon,
  coriander/cilantro

→ Seed and de-stem
  chilies
→ Soak chilies in water
  for half hour and
  reserve water
  for blending.
→ Blend until smooth.
→ Thin with chili water
  as needed.

Holy Moly Robin!
Guaca Mole

- 3 avocados
- 1 small red onion
- ¼ bunch cilantro
- juice of 1 lemon
- 1 tomato
- pinch of chili powder
- salt & pepper to taste

→ Dice onion, tomato
  and cilantro.
→ Mix items together
  by chopping with
  a paring knife.

TIP:
You can freeze
almost all of your
raw sauces without
losing too much
nutritional integrity.
Keep them
in a well-labeled
air-tight glass
container.

Great Bowls of Gravy
Groovy Gravy

- ½ cup young coconut water
- ½ cup pure water
- ¼ cup tahini
- 2 tbsp. nama shoyu
- 1 tbsp. lemon juice
- 1 clove of garlic
- 1 stalk celery
- ¼ small yellow onion
- 1 tbsp. yeast
- ¾ tsp. salt

→ Blend everything in high speed blender until smooth.

Suggestion

Add diced mushrooms for giblets.

Backyard Bonanza
BBQ sauce

- 1 cup sun-dried tomatoes
- 4 seeded tomatoes
- 2/3 cup cider vinegar
- ¼ cup blackstrap molasses
- ¼ small yellow onion
- 3 cloves garlic
- 2 tbsp. nama shoyu
- 2 tbsp. agave
- 1 tbsp. yeast
- 1 tbsp. chili powder
- pinch of cayenne pepper (optional)

→ Soak sun-dried tomatoes for ten minutes. Reserve water for blending.

→ Blend all ingredients in high speed blender until smooth.

→ Thin with tomato water as needed.

Catch Up
Ketchup

- 1 cup sun-dried tomatoes
- 2 seeded tomatoes
- ¼ cup cider vinegar
- 2 tbsp. nama shoyu
- 2 tbsp. agave
- 1 clove garlic
- salt to taste

→ Soak sun-dried tomatoes for ten minutes. Reserve water for blending.
→ Blend until smooth.

Suggestion
Serve immediately or dehydrate 2-4 hours to thicken.
BONUS: try fermenting your ketchup...
but that's a whole 'nother book!

Hold the Pickles
Mayonnaise

- 1 cup olive oil
- ½ cup almonds
- 3 tbsp. lemon juice
- 1 tbsp. cider vinegar
- 1 tbsp. yeast
- 1 tbsp. lecithin (optional thickener)
- 1 clove garlic
- salt to taste

→ Blend in high speed blender until smooth.

Suggestion
Substitute cashews for almonds.

Pining for Pasta
Pesto Sauce

- 1 cup pine nuts
- ¼ cup lemon juice
- 3 tbsp. olive oil
- 1 cup basil
  (packed down)
- 3 cloves garlic
- ½ tsp. salt

→ Throw everything
in food processor
and blend until
smooth.

Suggestion
Garnish with additional
pine nuts and basil
leaves.
Top with Nutty Topping.
(Page 32).

TIP:
Find lots of
Noodle ideas
on Page 48.

Sweet & Sour
Teriyaki Sauce

- ¼ cup nama shoyu
- ¼ cup maple syrup
- ¼ thumb ginger
- ½ clove garlic

→ Blend all ingredients
in high speed blender
until smooth.

Me So Corny
Miso Dressing

- Juice of 1 lemon
- ½ cup raw tahini
- ¼ cup sesame oil
- 1 tbsp. yellow miso
- ¼ cup water (used
  as needed to blend)

→ Blend until smooth.

Crusts of Bread & Such

Raw breads and crusts are probably the most time intensive of raw food preparation. Items with nuts and seeds will require pre-soaking before and dehydration after. But if you know this going in, it will make the transition easier.

If you don't have the patience to make your own breads, there are raw wraps and crackers available at some health food stores.

There is a product line in your frozen food section of your health food store which is baked at low temperatures that you can use in a pinch.

Or if you must have bread, look for sprouted grain breads. But I have to tell you that there is nothing as rewarding as making your own RAW bread.

Sammy Time!
Basic Almond Bread

- Almond Flour (Page 76)
- salt to taste

→ Use as much or as little flour as you have or need.

→ Blend flour with salt and use just enough water to blend.

→ Spread on teflex sheets.

→ Dehydrate ½ day.

Suggestions

Make a simple snack by putting a slice of avocado on raw bread with a spritz of nama shoyu on top. →

Add fresh rosemary sprigs or minced garlic to any bread to make it extra special.

To make any sandwich really swing - a slice of tomato is tops.

Ollie, How I Luv Ya. How I Luv Ya.
Olive Bread

- 2 ½ cups walnuts
- 1 cup pitted olives
- ½ cup flax meal
- 4 tbsp. olive oil
- pinch of salt

→ Blend in food processor.

→ Spread on teflex sheets ¼ thick.

→ Dehydrate one day.

→ Flip halfway through to ensure both sides dry properly.

Stick it to Me
Cheese Bread Sticks

- 2 cup sunflower seeds
- ¼ cup nama shoyu
- 2 tbsp. yeast
- juice of 1 lemon
- 2 cloves garlic

→ Blend ingredients in food processor.

→ Spread mixture on teflex sheets like long straws or sticks

→ Dehydrate ½ day.

→ Flip halfway through the dehydration, so underside dehydrates.

Suggestions

Blend less for chunkier cheese.

Sprinkle on additional yeast and/or minced sunflower seeds to give the sticks more 'texture.'

Blend in a seeded jalapeño or a red bell pepper.

Don't Cry for Me
Onion Bread

- 3 sweet onions
- 1 cup sunflower seeds
- 1 cup flax meal
- ½ cup olive oil
- 1/3 cup nama shoyu

→ Slice onions thinly.

→ Mix all ingredients in big bowl.

→ Spread on teflex sheets approximately ¼" thick.

→ Dehydrate one day.

→ Flip halfway through.

Suggestions

Serve with sliced avocado on top.

Trusty Crust
Pizza Crust

- 2 cups walnuts
- 2 cups zucchini (peeled)
- ½ cup flax meal
- ¼ cup sesame seeds
- ¼ cup water
- ¼ cup agave
- ½ lemon (trim rind)
- salt to taste

→ Blend in food processor.
→ Spread on teflex sheets approximately ⅛" thick.
→ Dehydrate 8-10 hours.
→ Flip halfway through.

Suggestions

Top off crust with Marinara Sauce (Page 35).

Add a slice of raw or vegan cheese and a sprig of basil and voila! Raw pizza! →

Gaga for Garlic
Sour Dough
Garlic Bread

- ¾ cup flax meal
- ¾ cup sunflower seed
- ½ cup nama shoyu
- ⅓ cup olive oil
- ¼ cup yeast
- 4 cloves garlic
- 1 lemon (trim rind)

→ Blend in food processor.
→ Spread on teflex tray about ¼" thick.
→ Dehydrate one day.
→ Flip halfway through.

Suggestion

Spread thicker on teflex and once dehydrated - break into Crouton size.

Corn to be Wild!
Corn Tortilla Chips

- 3-4 ears of raw corn (roughly 4 cups)
- ½ red bell pepper
- ¼ cup flax meal
- juice of 1 lemon
- 2 tbsp. minced onion
- 1 tsp. salt
- ½ tsp. turmeric

→ Cut corn off cob and seed pepper.

→ Blend until smooth. Add water to thin mixture as needed.

→ Spread thinly on teflex sheet. Sprinkle with additional salt.

→ Dehydrate 6 hours.

→ Flip, lightly score, and sprinkle with additional salt.

→ Dehydrate 4 hours.

Suggestions

Serve with Salsa (Page 37) or Guacamole (Page 39)

Everything It's Cracked Up to Be
Herb Crackers

- ½ cup flax meal
- ½ cup water
- 1 tsp. nama shoyu
- 1 tbsp. (altogether) of seasonings: parsley, sage, rosemary and thyme
  OR
  1 tbsp. sliced olives
  OR
  1 tbsp. sesame seeds

→ Blend flax, water and nama shoyu and ½ of seasonings in food processor.

→ Spread on teflex sheets and mix in remaining seasonings into the mixture as you spread it out.

→ Dehydrate ½ day

→ Flip halfway through and score lightly.

TIPS:
There are gadgets known as 'spiroli.' They make noodles out of Zucchini or other veggies.
If you start to miss pastas and noodles on your raw diet, these things will save your life.

Get a "Cutting Glove" to protect your fingers!

It may seem daunting at first, but you'll get the hang of it.
Use any of the following to make 'raw' noodles.

- **Zucchini Noodles with Marinara Sauce →(Page 35) my favorite!**
- **Rutabagas**
- **Beets**
- **Carrots**
- **Spaghetti Squash**

Spiral Sensations
Noodle Ideas

- **coconut meat**

→ Drain young coconut water and reserve for drinking or other recipes.

→ Crack open the young coconut and scoop out the innards.

→ Cut into long thin slices.

Suggestions
Serve 'noodles' with Marinara Sauce (Page 35), Peanut Sauce (Page 37), Alfredo Sauce (Page 36), or Pesto Sauce (Page 42)

Salads, Sides & Sustenance

I used to hate it when I would ask people where a good place to eat vegetarian food was, and they would reply, "Oh this or that place has good salads."

I would think... Vegetarianism doesn't mean you only eat salads, you know... But now that I am eating more raw food, I look forward to finding places that serve good salads!

But still, a raw régime doesn't begin and end with salads... There are many wonderful combinations of foods you can put together, from nut patties to pates! And if you get stuck in a raw rut, don't be afraid to mix in some lightly cooked foods with your meals. It's okay to have a little steamed broccoli or other parboiled items in with your raw ingredients.

You are limited only by your own imagination.

PanAsian Invasion

<u>Chinese Chickyless Salad</u>

- 1 head romaine
- 2 carrots
- ½ cup snap peas
- ½ cup almonds
- 2-3 scallions
- 3 tbsp. sesame seeds
- Chinese Chicky Dressing (Page 35)

→ Rinse and drain romaine lettuce.

→ Cut lettuce into 1 inch wide strips.

→ Shred carrots and chop almonds and onions.

→ Toss ingredients with dressing.

→ Sprinkle onions and sesame seeds on top.

Suggestions
Add lightly steamed broccoli florets.
Add diced Chicky Nuggets (Page 28).

It Slices! It Dices!

<u>Chopped Salad</u>

- 2 cobs corn
- 1 yellow or orange bell pepper
- 3 roma tomatoes
- 1 cup green beans
- 1 red onion
- 2 small zucchinis
- 2 small carrots
- 1 stalk celery
- 1 avocado
- drizzle of olive oil
- salt & pepper to taste

→ Cut corn off cob and dice up everything else and toss it all together.

→ This salad has so much flavor it does not need "dressing" - just a little oil, salt and pepper on top.

Suggestion
A squeeze of lemon will brighten up any sauce or dressing.
I recommend it!

A Pate on da Back
Walnut Pate

- 1 cup walnuts
- 1 zucchini
- ¼ cup olive oil
- juice of ½ lemon
- 1 clove garlic
- ½ tsp. onion powder
- 1 heaping tbsp. yeast
- 1 tsp raw miso
- salt to taste

→ Blend in food processor until smooth.

Suggestions
Mix in after blended: fresh chopped onion, celery and/or parsley

Cornball Style
Corn Salad

- 1 raw corn cob
- ½ red onion
- ½ cup diced tomato
- 1 bag of pre-washed arugula lettuce
- Italian Dressing (Page 33)

→ Cut the kernels off the corn with a very sharp knife.
→ Slice the onion thinly so that you have long ringlet curves of onion.
→ Toss with dressing.

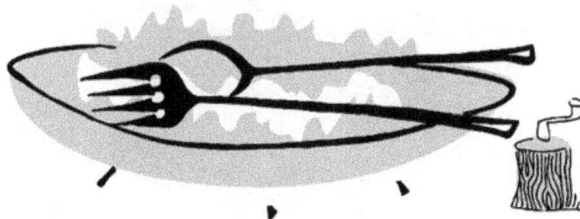

I Loves Olives
Tapenade

- 1½ cups pitted green olives
- ¼ cup olive oil
- 1 tbsp. lemon juice
- salt & pepper to taste

→ Pulse in food processor until ingredients are incorporated, but not smooth.

TIP:
To pit olives, put them on a cutting board and place a chef's knife over them flat side down. Gently hit the knife to expel the pit.

Extra Padding
Pad Thai Noodles

This is an advanced dish

- Coconut Noodles (Page 48)
- Peanut Sauce (Page 37)
- ½ cup bean sprouts
- ½ cup cabbage
- ½ cup carrots
- ½ cup jungle peanuts
- ¼ cup cilantro
- 3-4 sliced scallions
- 1 lime

→ Shred cabbage and carrots.

→ Chop cilantro and peanuts and slice scallions.

→ Toss noodles, carrots, cabbage, sprouts and sauce together.

→ Garnish with cilantro, peanuts, onions and lime wedge on top.

Great Greek
Greek Salad

- 1 cup Kalamata olives pitted
- 1 bell pepper
- 1 medium cucumber
- 1 tomato
- ½ red onion
- Greek Version of Italian Dressing (Page 33)
- 1 tsp fresh oregano

→ Rough chop red onion and bell pepper.

→ Dice cucumber.

→ Cut tomato into wedges.

→ Mix up ingredients with dressing.

→ Garnish with fresh oregano.

Parse the Parsley
Tabbouleh

- 2 tomatoes
- 1 bunch parsley
- 1 onion
- 1 small cucumber
- 1 cup lemon juice
- 1 handful mint
- ½ cup cauliflower
- 4 tbsp. olive oil
- salt & pepper to taste

→ Finely chop parsley and cauliflower.

→ Dice tomatoes, onions, cucumber and mint.

→ Combine all ingredients.

Suggestion

Serve with Raw Hummus (Page 36)

TIPS:
While cooking food will lower its nutrient density, lightly steaming cruciferous vegetables is considered acceptable on the raw food regime, because it may make them easier to digest.

Another way to help your cruciferous veggies become more digestible is to "massage" them, literally!

Take your kale, collard, or other thick greens and mush them up with your hands before serving.

Ultra Fini Brocolini
Italian Broccoli Salad

- 1 bunch broccolini
- juice of 2 lemons
- ½ red pepper
- 4 cloves garlic minced
- ¼ cup olive oil
- salt & pepper to taste

→ Slice and then marinate pepper the night before in lemon juice and salt.

→ Lightly steam broccolini for about 3 minutes and immediately blanch in ice water.

→ Make dressing from oil, lemon, garlic, salt and pepper.

→ Serve it up.

Tomato Onion Twist Twist

Tomato Onion Salad

- 4 ripe organic tomatoes
- 2 sweet Vidalia or Hawaiian onions
- 1+ cups cherry tomatoes
- 3 tbsp. olive oil
- 2 tbsp. cider vinegar
- salt & pepper to taste

→ Dice tomatoes.

→ Slice onions into ⅛" rings.

→ Mix ingredients in a big non-metal bowl.

→ Dress with oil and vinegar. The juice from the tomatoes will make most of the dressing.

Suggestions

Add ⅛ cup chopped basil.
Add ⅛ cup pine nuts.

TIP:
Please cut cherry tomatoes in half. This allows them to soak up the flavor of your dressing and makes it so they don't explode in your mouth when you eat them!

TIPS:
When spreading out bread or cracker 'dough' in your dehydrator, experiment with thickness, shapes and texture.
Spread crackers thinly using fork tongs.
Spread burger patties with a spoon back into thick round shapes.

Use a pizza cutter to lightly score breads into clean shapes while the dough is still pliable, about halfway through the dehydration process.

Hold the Bun
Burger Patties

This is an advanced dish

- 1 cup sunflower seeds
- 1 cup walnuts
- 1-2 stalks celery
- 1 medium zucchini
- ½ cup almonds
- ½ cup nama shoyu
- ½ cup flax meal
- ½ onion
- 2 tbsp. oil
- 4-5 cloves garlic
- ½ cup parsley (stems removed)

→ Mix all ingredients in food processor.
→ Form into patties on teflex sheet.
→ Dehydrate 12+ hours.
→ Flip and dehydrate another 12+ hours.

Suggestion
Roll into one inch balls and dehydrate to make "Neat-o Balls" and serve with Marinara Sauce (Page 35).

Soup 'n' Stuff

Raw food doesn't strictly mean cold food! If you use a commercial blender, you will find that the friction caused by mixing for a while will actually heat up your ingredients. And when a recipe calls for water, you can simply use HOT water to make a warm soup!

Also, if your food is ice cold, you could still heat things up using a low flame and a pot. Raw food enzymes remain intact up to roughly 118 degrees wet. You can actually heat things up a wee bit more provided it is for a very short time. And since 118 degrees is hotter than the inside of your mouth, everything will taste warm to you.

But mainly, isn't it good to know - you will *never* burn your tongue or the roof of your mouth again!

Red Hots
Chili

- 2 tomatoes
- 1 onion
- ¾ cup sprouted lentils
- ½ red bell pepper
- 2 tbsp. scallions
- 2 tbsp. lemon juice
- 2 tbsp. nama shoyu
- 1 tbsp. olive oil
- 1 tsp. chili powder
- 1 tsp. cumin
- 1-2 cloves garlic
- Salt to taste

→ Rough chop as needed.

→ Pulse in food processor until chunky.

→ Then scoop out about two tbsp. and set aside.

→ Pulse more and then recombine.

Suggestions
Add Cayenne for Kick!
Garnish with additional red or white onions.

Shrooms Dude
Mushroom Soup

This is an advanced dish

- 3 cups portabella or crimini mushrooms
- 1 cup unsweetened Almond Milk (Page 76)
- 1 cup boiling water
- 3 stalks celery
- 4 cloves garlic
- ½ lemon (trim rind)
- ¼ cup olive oil
- 1 tsp. salt
- 1 minced mushroom

→ Blend all ingredients until smooth and stir in minced mushroom at the end.

TIP:
Remember that mushrooms are literally "fungus" Eat them sparingly and you can try them medicinally!

Life Saving Soup
Gazpacho

- 6 tomatoes
- 1 bell pepper
- 1 cucumber OR
  1 zucchini
- 1 avocado sliced
- ½ cup basil or cilantro
- ⅓ cup cider vinegar
- ¼ cup olive oil
- 1 tsp. nama shoyu
- 2 cloves of garlic
- salt & pepper to taste

→ Reserve half of:
  bell pepper, avocado
  and cucumber.

→ Blend the rest
  of the ingredients in
  blender until smooth.

→ Dice reserved pepper
  and cucumber.

→ Mix in soup and
  garnish with avocado
  and basil or cilantro.

TIP:
Do not over-blend
tomatoes or they
will tend to foam.

Youza Youza
Hot Tomato Soup

- 6 tomatoes
- 4 sun-dried tomatoes
- 1 cup boiling water
- ¼ teaspoon salt
- 1-2 cloves garlic
- 20 cashews

→ Soak sun-dried
  tomatoes for ten
  minutes.

→ Blend all ingredients
  in high speed blender.

→ Serve with raw
  crackers or croutons.

TIP:
Chop off the ends
(sprout and tip)
of your onion and
quickly throw them
in a closed waste
can at the opposite
end
of the room.
Then grab your
'open' ended onions
and immediately
peel the entire skin
under water.

As long as you work
quickly you may
never shed
a tear over
onions again.

TIP:
Raw food does not
have to be cold
when you make raw
soups blended with
hot water!

C'est Manifique
French Onion

- 1½ cups young coconut water
- 1½ cups boiling water
- 1 small onion
- 1 lemon (trim rind)
- ¼ cup olive oil
- ¼ cup nama shoyu
- 2 cloves garlic

→ Chop onion and marinate in nama shoyu minimum one hour or more.

→ Blend all ingredients until smooth.

Suggestions

Place onion rings (Page 30) on for a nice chewy topper. Garnish with garlic croutons. (Page 46).

Suggestions

Serve over peas, corn,
diced red pepper, carrots,
scallions, green beans,
broccoli,
and/or cooked potatoes.

Home-Made Curry Powder

Mix up your own
powders to make
a special home-made
curry powder

- **5 parts coriander**
- **2 parts turmeric**
- **2 parts cumin**
- **1 part ginger**
- **½ part garlic powder**
- **½ part cinnamon**
- **½ part clove powder**
- **½ part cardamom**
- **½ part nutmeg**

Suggestion

Also try fennel, mace,
white pepper, and
fenugreek.

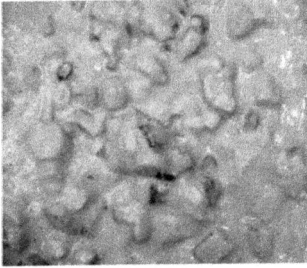

Not in a Hurry? Try Some Curry
Vegetable Curry Sauce

- **1 cup young coconut juice**
- **1 cup boiling water**
- **1 cup cashews**
- **1 cup coconut meat**
- **1 cup celery**
- **½ cup chopped cashews**
- **2 tbsp. agave**
- **1 tbsp. curry powder**
- **1 tbsp. turmeric powder**
- **1-2 garlic cloves**
- **1 thumb ginger**
- **salt to taste**

→ Reserve chopped cashews.
→ Blend all other ingredients until smooth.
→ Add chopped cashews.

Simply Smashing!
Spicy Split Pea Soup

This is an advanced dish

- **10 oz. bag of frozen unsalted peas OR 1 cup fresh English**
- **1 cup boiling water**
- **½ onion**
- **¼ cup nama shoyu**
- **¼ cup carrots**
- **2 dried chipotle chilies**
- **1 stalk celery**
- **1 clove garlic**
- **Salt to taste**
- **½ tsp. paprika**

→ Thaw peas if frozen.

→ Reserve ⅛ cup peas to add in later.

→ Seed and stem chilies and soak for 1/2 hour.

→ Chop onion and marinate in nama shoyu one hour or more.

→ Puree all, except for reserved peas.

→ After smooth, add in peas and pulse in.

Suggestions

Reserve a few carrots, finely chop them, and add in later for more texture.

If chipotles are too spicy for you, you could use liquid smoke to add that smoky flavor.

Eat Like Eve by Cherry Capri

Cookies & Dough

Now we are getting to my favorite section of things to make. I am hopelessly in love with making sweets and desserts for my friends (and myself). Luckily, with the raw food regime - they actually recommend that you *eat sweets FIRST!* This is because the sugary acids in desserts supposedly setup your stomach to digest food better.

Now, this is for me! Chocolate now! Salads later!

The other good thing about raw sweets is that the ingredients have so many beneficial components to them, you never have to feel too guilty about eating the entire plate of cookies or pint of ice cream; because after all, you also just ingested loads of live vitamins, enzymes and minerals, too. It's the ultimate justification diet! So just like
I advise to have raw snacks around, likewise, keep some cookies on hand, too.

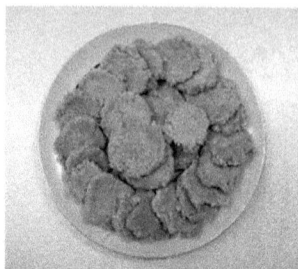

Poppies... That will sooth them
Lemon Cookies

- **2 cups Almond Flour (Page 76)**
- **2 whole lemons (sweet Meyers preferred)**
- **1 cup agave**
- **1 cup cashews**
- **1-2 tbsp. poppy seeds**
- **1 tsp. vanilla extract**
- **1 tsp. lemon extract**
- **½ tsp. salt**

→ Blend all ingredients together except for poppy seeds.

→ Transfer to bowl and blend in poppy seeds.

→ Spread tbsp. lumps on teflex tray.

→ Dehydrate one day.

→ Flip and press and flatten your cookies about halfway through the dehydration.

Living Well is the Sweetest
Basic Cookie Dough

- **1 cup Almond Flour (Page 76)**
- **¼ cup agave/honey**
- **½ tsp. salt**
- **2 tbsp. water**
- **1 tbsp. vanilla extract**
- **sprinkle of date sugar**

→ Blend all ingredients together in food processor until evenly wet - mixture will still be crumbly.

→ Scoop out tbsp. into your hand and roll into dough balls.

→ Put round balls on teflex tray

→ Dehydrate one day.

→ Halfway through, press flat and flip and add a sprinkle of date sugar on top for "sugar" cookies.

THE Essential
Chocolate Chip

- 1 cup cashews
- ¾ cup Almond Flour (Page 76)
- ½ cup agave
- ½ cup coconut butter
- ¼ cup raw cacao paste
- 1 tsp. vanilla
- 1 tsp. salt

→ Pulse in Food processer: cashews, agave, butter, vanilla, salt until NOT smooth (leave it nubby).

→ Break up cacao paste into tiny chunks.

→ Spoon blend "cacao paste chips" into mixture.

→ Roll into balls, flatten, and dehydrate one day. Flip and flatten more halfway thru.

Suggestion
Chocolate version add:
- ¼ cup cacao powder
- ¼ cup addl. agave

Hey Macaroona
Maple Maca Macaroons

- 1 heaping cup dried shredded coconut
- ½ cup maple syrup
- 1 tsp. maca powder
- 1 tsp. salt

→ Blend ingredients and let sit for an hour or two so the coconut soaks up the moisture of syrup.

→ Roll into 1" balls and dehydrate 5-6 hours. (Do not over dehydrate or you'll have crunchy macaroons).

TIP:
Raw Cookies may not taste like the baked cookies you are used to, but they still should satisfy cravings for: sugar, chocolate and fats.

Queen of Hearts
Basic Tart Crust

- 12 dates (pitted)
- ¾ cup coconut butter
- ½ cup pecans
- ½ tsp. vanilla extract
- ¼ tsp. each nutmeg, cinnamon, clove powder
- ¼ tsp. salt

→ Pulse in Food processor until blended. Dough should be crumbly but sticky enough to hold shape. Do not over-blend.

→ Press evenly into bottom and sides of container.

→ Refrigerate until ready to fill.

Suggestion

This will make one tart crust. Double recipe for a full pie crust. (But use less coconut butter.)

Fill with Chocolate Pudding, Lemon Cheesecake or 'Cooked' Apples (Chapter 8)

For a Natural High
RAWky Mountain Walnut Brownies

- 1½ cup cacao powder
- 1 cup Almond Flour (Page 76)
- 1 cup agave
- ½ cup walnuts
- ½ cup carob powder
- ½ cup coconut oil (or hemp oil!!!)
- ¼ cup maca
- 1 tsp. vanilla extract or seeds from bean
- pinch or two of salt

→ Blend everything except walnuts in food processor.

→ Lightly chop walnuts and spoon walnuts into mixture. (You may omit walnuts for just plain RAWkin' brownies.)

→ Spread in glass baking dish.

→ Dehydrate for one day - if you can wait that long.

Under my Thumb
Jam Thumbprints

This is an advanced dish

- 1 ½ cup Almond Flour (Page 76)
- ½ cup coconut butter
- ½ cup agave
- 1 tbsp. vanilla extract
- ¼ tsp. salt
- Berry Jam (Page 67)

→ Blend dough in food processor.

→ Place heaping tablespoonful's on teflex tray.

→ Dehydrate 4-6 hours. Then push thumbprint in middle.

→ Dehydrate 6-10 hours more.

→ Fill thumbprint holes with jam.

→ Dehydrate another hour or two so jam "sets."

In a Pickle
Berry Jam

- 1 cup fresh raspberries
- ½ cup dates pitted

→ Thaw berries if frozen.

→ Blend with dates in food processor.

Suggestions

You can also make strawberry jam, I prefer raspberries, because strawberries are quite hybridized.

You can sweeten your jam with agave, but it will be more like a sauce. To make it more jam-like, you will need to dehydrate it a bit.

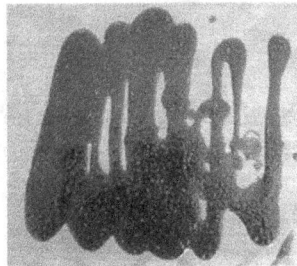

Delish
Desserts

You jumped to this chapter, didn't you?
Now let's really get down to brass tacks.
THIS is what you came for...

Natural raw treats seem to affect your whole body
differently. I have a supply of raw chocolate in my
freezer 24 hours a day, 7 days a week, without fail. I
like to entice my friends into the
raw habit by giving them a taste of what
I consider to be the healthiest SuperFood Sweet on
earth. RAWkin' Chocolate!

So let's get started!

Food for the Goddesses
Chocolate Pudding

- 2 cups young coconut meat
- ¾ cup coconut water
- ½ cup agave
- ½ cup cacao powder
- 2 tbsp. vanilla extract
- pinch of salt

→ Blend until smooth.
→ Store in fridge, IF there is any left to store!

Heaven. I'm in Heaven...
Chocolate Ice Cream

- Chocolate Pudding (Page 69)
- handful of cacao nibs

→ Follow previous directions, but then...
→ Process in ice cream maker.
→ Freeze and serve.
→ Sprinkle nibs on top.

Say Lemony
<u>Lemon Cheesecake</u>

This is an advanced dish

- **1 cup cashew butter (or enough soaked cashews to make cup of butter)**
- **¾ cup lemon juice**
- **¾ cup honey/agave**
- **4 dates pitted**
- **1 tsp. vanilla extract**
- **pinch of salt**
- **Tart Crust (Page 66)**

→ Blend soaked cashews to make
the 1 cup of butter.

→ Blend everything
in high speed blender.

→ Spoon into pie crust

→ Let set in fridge
overnight.

Suggestion

Make it a Chocolate Cheesecake by adding a ⅓ cup of raw cacao powder.
Serve with a Berry Coulis (Page 70).

Raw Food Been
Berry Berry Good
<u>Berry Coulis</u>

- **1 pint strawberries or raspberries**
- **¼ cup ice water**
- **¼ cup agave**

→ Blend everything
in high speed blender.

Suggestion

Serve with Chocolate Cheesecake (Page 70) or with RAWkin' Brownies (Page 66).

TIP:
Be careful, frozen cacao 'nibs' get as hard as rocks.

RAWkin' RAWket Chocolate

Dark Chocolate

- **3 cups cacao powder**
- **2 cups almond butter**
- **2 cups soft coconut oil**
- **1 cup carob powder**
- **1 cup agave**
- **1 tsp. vanilla extract**
- **1 tsp. salt**

→ Blend together in stand mixer.

→ Spread in bottom of baking dish(s) at approximately ½" thickness.

→ Store in freezer to keep hardened.

Suggestions

This is a LARGE batch meant to last you awhile and enough to share with friends!

Add peppermint oil, softened coconut shreds, chopped almonds or macadamias.

Add pureed raspberries.

TIP:
For more 'tactile' chocolate, grind raw cacao nibs in a coffee grinder to a very fine powder (or it will be gritty). You can reduce the oils in the recipe because cacao butter will be released from the nibs.

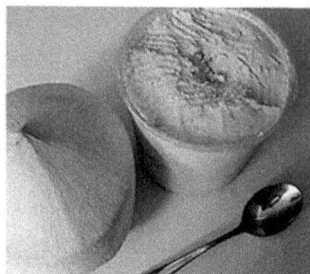

I'm Koo Koo for Coconuts
Coconut Ice Cream

- juice and meat of 2-3 young coconuts
- 1 cup agave
- pinch of salt

→ Blend in food processor until smooth.

→ Process in ice cream maker.

→ Freeze and serve.

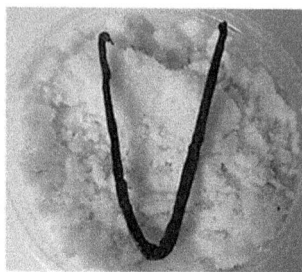

I Scream for More
Vanilla Ice Cream

- 1 cup cashews (must be soaked)
- 1 ½ cups young coconut meat
- 2 cups water
- 1 cup agave
- ½ cup coconut butter
- 2 vanilla beans (or 4 tbsp. vanilla extract)
- pinch of salt

→ Blend in food processor until smooth.

→ Process in ice cream maker.

→ Freeze and serve.

Suggestions

Add peppermint oil, plus some extra agave, and chunks of cacao paste for a mint chip.

Add a swirl of maple syrup or honey and sugared pecans for Pralines & Cream.

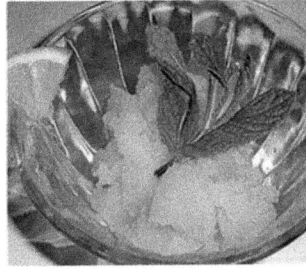

Banana Splits
Strawberry Ice

- 1 cup strawberries
- 1 cup bananas
- ½ cup agave

→ Blend everything
  in high speed blender
→ Process in
  ice cream maker.
→ Freeze and serve.

Suggestions

Make frozen fruit
ices and sorbets
out of whatever
fresh fruits are
in season.
Try raspberries,
blueberries,
blackberries
or whatever fruit suits
your fancy!

Lemony Heaven
Lemon Ice

- 1 cup lemon juice
- 1 cup agave/honey
- 3 cups water

→ Blend everything
  in high speed blender.
→ Process in
  ice cream maker.
→ Freeze and serve.

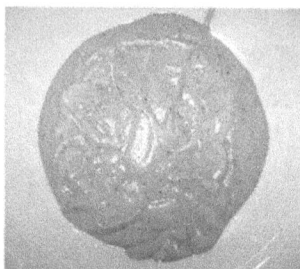

Mommy Eve's Dish
Apple Tart

This is an advanced dish

- 3 apples
- ½ cup dates pitted
- 1 tsp. cinnamon
- 1 tsp. allspice
- ½ tsp nutmeg
- juice of 3 lemons
- Tart Crust (Page 66)

→ Slice 2 apples using a vegetable peeler.

→ Marinate apple slices in juice of 2 lemons overnight. Discard lemon juice later.

→ Puree 1 apple, dates, and juice of 3rd lemon and all the spices.

→ Mix marinated apples with sauce. Put in pie crust and refrigerate.

TIP:
Use lemon juice to "cook" almost anything by marinating it overnight!

Whip it Good
Cashew Cream

- 1 cup young coconut meat
- 3 tbsp. cashews or macadamia nuts
- ½ cup agave
- 3 tbsp. young coconut water or almond milk
- ½ tsp. lemon zest
- 1 vanilla bean
- pinch of salt

→ Blend in high speed blender until creamy.

→ Cool down in fridge and serve.

Suggestions

→ Use Cashew Cream as a topping on Chocolate Pudding (Page 69), Lemon Cheesecake (Page 70) or Apple Pie (Page 74) OR even on top of a *cooked desert* to get enzymes going!

Drinks &
Smoothies

Want to get thin and super healthy faster?
Then follow the old adages of increasing your
metabolism through diet and exercise.
They do seem to work!

And when you watch what you eat, raw liquids
make perfect sense to me for the "diet" part.
This is because you are feeding yourself tons
of nutrients very quickly and making them easier to
assimilate. So your body says, "Speed up that
metabolism to burn off all this stuff coming in."
But at the same time, there is not a lot of fat
or oil to clog up the system and add pounds.

Just remember to CHEW your juice!

Joy to the Almonds!
Almond Milk

- 3 cup water
- 1 cup almonds
- pinch of salt

→ Blend water and almonds until smooth.

→ Strain through nut milk bag, or cheese cloth (or paint strainer bag from hardware store).

→ Set this pulp aside for Almond Flour.

→ Re-blend with pinch of salt.

→ Chill and serve.

Suggestions

Remember to always pre-soak the almonds overnight or at least a few hours.

For more nutrition – add a couple of tsp. of hemp seed oil into the mix.

Sweetened Vanilla Variation

After straining, add:
- ¼ cup agave
- seeds from vanilla bean, or a ¼ tsp. of vanilla extract
- pinch of salt to taste

Chocolate Variation

After straining, add:
- ¼ cup cacao powder
- ½ cup agave
- pinch of salt to taste

Chai Variation

After straining, add:
- pinches of cinnamon, cardamom, nutmeg, clove powders and more agave.

Almond Flour

When you strain the nut milk, you will have a load of pulp leftover in your nut milk bag.

→ Spread this pulp out on a teflex tray.

→ Dehydrate for a day.

→ Once dried, grind in the food processor or coffee grinder to make a fine raw flour.

→ Store in an airtight glass container in your fridge or freezer and date it.

X-Egg
X-mas Treat
Eggless Nog

- 3 cups ice water
- 1 cup cashews
- 1 cup macadamia nuts
- 5 tbsp. agave
- 3 pinches of nutmeg
- salt to taste

→ Blend water, nuts, agave, salt and 2 pinches nutmeg really well until extra smooth.

→ Chill and serve.

→ Garnish with pinch of nutmeg on top.

Suggestion

You can add 1 tbsp. lecithin to make your nog thicker.

It's Easy Being...
Green Lemonade

- 3 leaves dark kale
- 3 apples
- 1 head romaine lettuce
- 1 entire lemon

→ Juice in juicer and serve over ice.

Jamaican Delight
Ginger Ale

- juice of 2 oranges
- juice of 1 lime
- 1 cup cold water
- 1" or more peeled
  thumb of ginger
- ½ cup ice
- 1-2 tbsp. agave/honey

→ Juice fruit
   and ginger in juicer.
→ Then blend
   in remaining
   ingredients.
→ Serve over ice.

Suggestion

If you do not have
a juicer, you can make
this in a blender,
you will just need
to strain out the ginger
and orange pulp.

I coulda had a...
Vegetable Delight

- 4 medium tomatoes
- 2 stalks celery
- ½ cucumber
  (I prefer English)
- juice of 1 lemon
- 2 cloves garlic
- 5-10 scallions
  (depending on size)
- 3 romaine leaves
- 1 small red pepper
  (seeded)
- 1 ½ cups cold water
- salt & pepper to taste

→ Blend in high speed
   blender until smooth.
→ Slap your forehead
   when you forget
   to make this drink!

Mister Clean
Spicy Lemonade

- juice of 1 lemon
- 1 tbsp. agave/honey
- 2 cups water
- $^1/_8$ tsp. cayenne pepper (more or less)

→ Mix together ingredients and serve over the rocks.

Suggestion

The "Master Cleanse" spicy lemonade calls for Grade B Maple Syrup, however,
I prefer to use honey (not vegan) as it contains even more of certain beneficial nutrients. Add 1 tbsp. liquid chlorophyll or green powders for Bonus Nutrition Points.

Healthier for Hemmingway
Mint - Lime Mojito

- 2 limes juiced
- ¼ cup agave
- 2 cups ice water
- handful of mint leaves

→ Muddle mint, lime and agave at the bottom of a glass.

→ Add ice and water and stir.

→ Garnish with slice of lime.

Orange you Glad?
50-50 Shake

- 1 cup fresh squeezed orange juice
- 1 cup sweetened vanilla Almond Milk (Page 76)
- Ice

→ Blend until smooth.

TIP:
Who needs
a canned
'energy drink' when
you can get all
sorts of stimulus
and experience
RAW euphoria with
a Cacao Shake!

Monster Energy
Cacao Shake

- 2 cups cold water
- ½ cup cacao powder
- ¼ cup agave
- 1 tsp. vanilla extract
- pinch of salt
- ice

→ Blend until smooth.

Suggestions
Pump up any Cacao Shake with any or all of your fave additions:

- Carob Powder
- Cinnamon
- Goji Berries
- Green Powders
- Hemp Powder
- Lecithin
- Maca Powder
- Any of your favorite Superfood powders!

Postscript

Comfort Food Combos

k.d. lang once said... "Constant craving has always been...." I think she was singing about something else, but the concept does apply for foods.

For the most part, I have essentially eliminated many of my food cravings for the things I used to eat. But now and then I get the urge for an old favorite. That's when I either just give in and eat it and let it be, OR I get extra clever.

For instance, I take my Chicky Nuggets (Page 28) and crumble them and soak them in a layer of teriyaki sauce (Page 42) and serve them over some romaine lettuce... Voila!
Teriyaki Chicky Salad.

If you do break from your super healthy diet and still feel guilty eating cooked food, that's not going to help you out. If you eat some outrageous 'naughty' cooked foods, please enjoy them and *relish them*. Then go back to relishing your healthy foods with the same gusto. Allow yourself to enjoy the foods you like while putting the Raw Food "training wheels" on and just get going!

Remember that you can substitute raw sauces for any cooked ones. For instance, raw curry over cooked rice or raw marinara or raw Alfredo over cooked pasta. Yes, it's 50% cooked, but that's also 50% raw! Much better than 100% cooked. I do this often - especially in the winter time when I tend to crave more 'warming' foods.

Raw Vegetable Curry (Page 61) over long grain wild rice and Raw Alfredo (Page 36) sauce over gluten-free spaghetti.

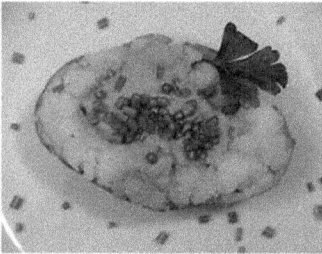

Raw Gravy (Page 40) and chives over a baked potato and Raw Meatballs (Page 56) and Raw Marinara (Page 35) served on a toasted organic sourdough gluten-free bun.

Also remember that many traditional ethnic dishes from across the globe, especially from the Mediterranean region, are already mostly raw! So just make and eat more of those. Hopefully, you will have enough basic recipes in this book that you can mix and match to find just the right combo to suit your craving.

And remember, keep things simple... Easy Does It.

Additional Preparation Notes

I have not listed portion sizes intentionally.
The recipes make enough for 1-2 people to share. And
the raw regime is not about counting calories or
portion control, so just release that mind set,
at least for this book.

You may also notice that some of the instructions
may seem a bit nebulous. I want to encourage you to
have faith in yourself and to trust your instincts.
Cooking is not a science, as some people would have
you believe. Sure, there are some scientific
principles involved in the chemistry,
but it is more of an art. And you are the artist! There
really are no mistakes in raw food preparation, just
unusual or exotic results.

These recipes are meant as a launching point.
Feel free to experiment. Adjust them to your
personal taste. If Chef Mason had it his way, there
would be cayenne in every recipe in this book! ☺

Use *all* of your senses, not just taste:
How does your dish look? How does the dish smell?
How does it feel in your mouth?

Unlike cooked foods, you can always adjust your
creations after you have 'supposedly' completed the
process. Raw foods are very forgiving. It's not like
you baked a pie and it's a done deal. You can scoop
out the filling and adjust whatever it needs and
dehydrate or freeze a second time.

In the very worst case scenario and you have made
something that is completely unpalatable, Huzzah! It
can always end up as useful compost
to grow your next batch of living food. It's a cycle
that never ends. So remain calm and elude
frustration. Love the time you spend shopping
for food and making it. You CAN do it.

And know that I, Cherry Capri, believe in you 100%.

Final Words

Since you have made it this far, I am going to use this last page to lay a little philosophy on you and offer you a challenge. Try to eat a little lower on the food chain and a little closer to Eden and see if it doesn't have profound effects on the rest of your life.

After being vegetarian for a while, I started to have more empathy for others. After going totally raw, I personally found I had more patience and was just plain happier. For your mind and spirit to be in alignment, you need your body temple to be in tip top shape. I personally believe all mental, emotional and spiritual healing begins with *physical healing*. Cleanse the body and the mind will follow. A healthy body is the foundation for the rest of your happy life.

The Garden of Eden must have been a very peaceful place to live. There was abundance everywhere...

And nobody was eating anybody else!

I believe that if we "act as if" we can start to recreate that same Eden feeling by making different choices in our lives. We *can* change the way we look at the world - through the way we treat our bodies.

Sure, in the bible, Eve was asked to leave Eden, but there's no reason why we all can't do our due diligence and eat our way back in!

Cheers to your health!

Cherry Capri ™

Resources

I own literally tons of books on healthy food and healing (not to mention tons more books on vintage and pop culture)! Here are the ones that I seem to reference often.

You can go to my website to get links to these items: www.cherrycapri.com

Books that Helped Me Get Started
Eating for Beauty by David Wolfe
The Raw Food Detox Diet by Natalie Rose

Thinking Differently About Healthy Food
12 Steps to Raw Food by Victoria Boutenko
Fats that Heal Fats that Kill by Udo Eramus
Hippocrates Life Force by Brian Clement NMD
Spiritual Nutrition by Gabriel Cousens, MD
Soak Your Nuts by Karyn Calabrese
Survival in the 21st Century by Viktoras Kulvinskas
The Raw Food Nutrition Handbook by Karin Dina, DC
Wild Fermentation by Sandor Katz

Recipe Books
Love on a Plate by Cara Brotman & Markus Rothkranz
Raw Food Revolution Diet by Cherie Soria
Raw Food Real World by Matthew Kenney
   & Sarma Melngailis
Rawvolution by Matt Amsden
Sweet Gratitude by Matthew Rogers
   & Tiziana Alipo Tamborra

Additional Tools
I find these tools to be helpful in getting work done:
Eco Peaceful organic nut milk bags (ecopeaceful.com)
Coco Jack for opening coconuts (coco-jack.com)

Index

This index is set up so that if you have this item, you can find a recipe that calls for it:

About the Author: Cherry Capri

Cherry Capri is a quirky red haired performance artist and pop cult celebrity. She is YOUR eccentric Auntie Mame whose world is full of vintage style with bossa nova and surf music, retro futurism and Rat Pack era shenanigans. Cherry is known for her outrageous recycled pink polyester pantsuits. For over ten years, Cherry has written a *"Dear Cherry"* advice column for <u>CA Modern Magazine</u> and formerly for <u>Bachelor Pad Magazine</u> and <u>Tiki Magazine</u>. Her column focuses on healthy homemaking and hosting, eco-friendly decorating along with Modern manners.

Remember to request her weekly *"Dear Cherry"* radio drop-in shows from Public Radio Exchange!

As a performer, Cherry has headlined three *Mondo Lounge* shows and the *Mondo Tiki* event at the Hard Rock Hotel. She has performed at tiki clubs across the country. Cherry is also a sculptor and painter who's exhibited in Hollywood, Las Vegas, Palm Springs and San Francisco in one women shows and alongside Shag and other luminaries of the Southern California Pop Surrealist scene. Always known to pay respect to her elders, the cover of her collectible album *"Creamy Cocktails & Other Delights"* featured a fun homage to the classic *"Whipped Cream"* album by Herb Alpert.

Finally, Cherry Capri was once crowned QUEEN of the famous *Pasadena Doo Dah Parade!* So is it any wonder that Cherry Capri is known as *America's Mistress of Modernism, Manners & Mirth!?* It is her mission in life to spread the joy of Mid-Mod Living combined with a hip healthy attitude!

www.cherrycapri.com
Facebook.com/DearCherryCapri

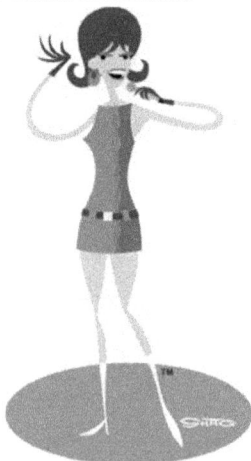

Co-Author, Anand

UCLA grad, Mary-Margaret Stratton, aka Anand, is a producer, UX architect and an award-winning Creative Director for the likes of DreamWorks, Tommy Bahamas
and Mattel Toys. She is the author of a self-help manual Stop Picking on Me, pagan primer the Good Wiccan, two tour guides on Mid-Mod architecture How Modern Was My Valley and Mondo Vegas, and editor of a Raw Food compendium called Powerful and Dominant Health.

Anand was certified as a Raw Food Nutritionist under David Wolfe at *Body Mind Institute*. She has been a vegetarian for over twenty years and primarily raw for the last ten years. In 2011, she was ordained as an Essene Minister. The Essenes are noted for their commitment to peace and a live food diet.

Co-Author, Chef Mason Green

Like fellow Raw Food educator, David Wolfe, Chef Mason Green (aka Cary Stratton) has been playing drums for most of his life. He is retired from the movie business after working on films such as Saving Private Ryan, Titanic, the Big Lebowsky and Austin Powers.

As a Chef, Mason graduated as a Certified Chef and Educator under Cherie Soria at *Living Light Culinary Arts Institute*. He has provided private chef-ing, catering and food styling for TV shows such as Glee and Community.

His recipes have been featured in CA Modern Magazine. Mason has been a vegetarian for over 20 years and primarily a raw foodie for half that time.

Photo by Bryan Hainer

In the beginning, Eve was running around
the Garden of Eden practically nude...
And she probably looked pretty darn good!

Miss Cherry Capri suggests
that the reason why Eve looked so good is
because she was eating a healthy
uncooked plant-based diet.
How could you not look great
if all you ate were organic fresh fruits,
nuts, seeds, greens and veggies?
That's the point of eating Raw Food. When
you eat dead flesh and overcooked foods,
you'll feel lousy and look
over-cooked! But eating Living Foods may
help you look and feel more alive!

In Eat Like Eve, pop culture
Modern Maven Cherry Capri introduces
you to 88 simple, delicious, fool-proof
dishes. They are easy to understand with
clear instructions and include color
photographs and time-saving
tips 'n' techniques. And in quintessential
Cherry style, this cookbook is filled with
fun fifties illustrations!

The recipes are vegan, gluten free,
and made from family-friendly all-natural
ingredients. So get back to the garden.
Step up to that tree.
EAT THAT APPLE!

And Eat Like Eve!

www.ingramcontent.com/pod-product-compliance
Lightning Source LLC
Chambersburg PA
CBHW071016040426
42443CB00007B/808